I0749883

HOW TO KILL YOURSELF INSTEAD OF YOUR CHILDREN

QUINCY SCOTT JONES

POETRY

C&R Press
Conscious & Responsible

Printed in the United States of America

First Edition
1 2 3 4 5 6 7 8 9

Cover Art Don't by Serafina Ye Jin Ha Kim (하예진)
Interior design by Jojo Rita

ISBN 978-1-949540-20-8
LCCN 2021939660

C&R Press
Conscious & Responsible
crpress.org

For special discounted bulk purchases, please contact:
C&R Press sales@crpress.org
Contact info@crpress.org to book events, readings and author signings.

HOW TO KILL YOURSELF INSTEAD OF YOUR CHILDREN

CONTENTS

If you're thinking about suicide, are worried about a friend or loved one, or would like emotional support, please use the number below.

National Suicide Prevention Lifeline

1-800-273-8255

For my wife

For my people

For all the parents taking slow breaths waiting for their kids to come home

sssssssssssssh. sssssssssssssssssh.
if you ssssssssssssh i'll tell you when

    we found the lynched boys
    restrung them in the leaves

hidden cherubs   /   tourist canopies
 we rehung them in the trees

        nobody knows
    they sing when it breeze

the neighborhood knows
ssssssssssssssh.

DON'T

Don't do that

Don't do that!
Don't talk back

Don't give me that look
Don't roll your eyes
You know what you did
Don't act surprised

Don't mismatch your clothes
Don't pull at a knot
Don't go near a window
If you hear a gun shot

Don't do what I do
Don't say what I say
Don't sit by yourself
On the docks by the bay

Don't dance to that hip-hop
Don't swing to no blues
Don't be waking-up the people
The people are hitting snooze

Don't say revolution
You're just going to lose
Find your picture posted
On the 11 o'clock news

Don't resist. Don't struggle
Don't put up a fight
Don't argue with the Policeman
Mr. Policeman's always right

Mr. Policeman has a gun
Mr. Gun has a sight
Mr. Bullet very fast
Mr. Coffin very tight

Don't write no letters
Don't post no bail
Everybody's guilty
That's why they're in jail

Don't embolden the enemy
Don't question the war
Don't blame "the president"
Ain't there no more

Don't charge your donation
Visa takes off the top
And the governments' corrupt
So maybe you should stop

Crying over Haiti Chile
DR Congo Jerusalem
North Philly West Philly
The Bottom Kensington

And don't drop a tear
For dry New Orleans
And don't wear silk stockings
With gold in the seams

Don't act too frigid
Don't make yourself a slut
Don't take New Jersey Transit
If you're half past drunk

Don't mess with them guys
They only want in your draws
Don't be alone with that girl
It's her word against yours

Don't offer a smile
Don't compliment her dress
Don't take a second look
They'll kill you for less

Don't think you're too good
To be back on your knees
Have you picking at the cotton
Swinging from the trees

Don't think times a changing
Don't think yes we can
This is still America
You still African

Or Asian or Irish
Just an N-word off the boat
If you doubt what I'm saying
Don't

ADVICE FROM THE STATUE ON MY MOTHER'S BOOKSHELF

Best keep your head down
Best do more studying
and less studying of me
Yes my right arm becomes the horse's
bridle and my left becomes the tail
I am both mount and rider
goddess and beast
just like everyone else.
Best race ahead of everyone
else. Best stop considering
whether I was carved
on the sands of Senegal or shipped
from an off-shore American assembly line.
I'm doing fine. How's that history book?
Best read it like it's your story.
Now it is.
If your ancestors wore shackles
don't follow with questions.
If they say you were animal
you say yes ma'm. Fill exam
books with answers already
provided. Keep your head down.
Keep yourself safe.
Best not think I'm a keepsake
bought for $48 at whatever
exchange rate wrapped in an
old scarf to keep safe by an
ex-boyfriend before he knew
he was an ex. Best keep to the text:
How the spice roads were all closed
and the mess the Moors made of Spain.
Don't even try to explain slavery
or Manifest Destiny
or 1807 men and women bound and sold

at whatever exchange rate
for horses and gold
who at St. George d'Elmina, the Gate
Of No Return,
would cup their hands
and swallow sand
until their stomachs burned
so they could always carry the motherland.
They're the least of your concerns.
Best buy what the school's selling you.
And best keep your head down
cause one look up – just one more look up –
and I'll bring this bookshelf down upon you.
Turn my rope arms to whips, make a man of letters out of you.
Raise the scars of your skin into lines of an epic.
Have your body misread for life.

HOW TO BE NICE

The first time a white boy calls you nigger
or calls out nigger while you are near
not knowing he's calling you out your name
your sisters' and brothers' and mother's mothers
don't be angry at your silence.
You are in shock

and you can always come back
to this later when you see him again.
You will see him again.
When you see him walk up
with a softness and come to him
with neither smile nor frown
take the back of his neck
like you would a newborn
and throw his head into a table.

A good table. Solid table.
I recommend wood.
Wood has a give and this is an act of giving.

Give him unconsciousness
so he can have a rest.
Give him a mark
so he will have something upon which to reflect.
Give him your all – a sharpness and strength
sequenced from centuries of dealing with this mess

and if you do it right
I mean do it just right
unlike you he won't even feel a thing.

HOW TO ACT YOUR AGE

If years are days at sea
my body would be a ship of death
and disease finally allowed to dock.
I feel no illness

or sickness other than what sticks
in my teeth. I lust
for the soft touch of dark chocolate
the sweet burn of sweet tea
the sweat of the night on the back
of my wife's knee or the curve of her thigh
and of course I crave rhyme.
Fight my craving for rhyme every time
I pick up my pen and all too often
I fail.

This poem's about teeth. That ship ain't coming back.

To dream of teeth falling out
is to dream of death
and at night my teeth
crumble from my lip
and with no dam to hold
it back my spit sick
and thick falls in long pours
like honey off a comb
until the comb is all bone
and there's no honey left.

This is not about death. This is about teeth.

And once when I was too young
to remember my mother took me
to a funeral and there on her knee

I asked Why is that man in a box
Mommy? and she said ssshh
he's sleeping. and I said Well
why doesn't someone wake him up?
and the whole church laughed
and laughed an ocean of Black
faces in black suits just showing

their teeth to the world.

HOW TO RECYCLE A WHITE PLASTIC BAG

that breathes when no one is looking
fills and falls like an *Amistad* sail
crashing on a New York shore.

no one is sure how it got there

skin of dust starting to form
the plastic bag models morning mist
in a dirty field
in an impoverished city
but refuses to burn itself off.

we thought it an allusion
allegory or metaphor
but after looking at it lie on the floor
we realized it was plastic bag.

the plastic bag sits there
          through the entire *Today* show.

the plastic bag fails to move
          like a civil rights bill.

the white plastic bag takes up more
and more of the apartment everyday
skews light in certain way
that makes everything less real
starts to feel like leftovers from restaurants
where my mother couldn't eat
and ways to pull bodies
of brothers off the street.

the white plastic speaks in dead languages
filthy with questions like
where you goin?

whatcha doin?
who you daddy is?

What's with this no ban biz?
Why don't they build a wall?
Who's Assata Shakur?
Why there police lights at the door?

once the plastic bag disappeared for four days
and you catching me looking at your legs
and you laughing at a joke in my shirt
and you ready to flirt with summer
 air coming through the lashes of our eyes.

the white plastic bag floats on by

lies itself in an empty corner
 quiet like a cancer.

we play Bid Whist for an answer
Maybe we should use it for our rotted books?
Maybe we should fill it with our heart pulp?
Maybe we should pull it over our heads?

instead we light candles for Davali
dance to bring back Africa
read aloud the *Uncanny X-men*
and watch the white melt

down to the rivers
down to the waters
down to our tears and the crack

in our bones until there
is no white
there is not even white

to be seen and everything
and everything and everything
is plastic.

KIDS WILL BE ?[i]

On November 22nd 2014
a Cleveland Police Officer shot 12 year old Tamir Rice

this was a justified shooting
learn from this incident

Your children should
not be allowed
throughout the neighborhood
guns have no warning
guns do have your child
These guns are very real

Warn them
The Police may get called to respond
it is important to know how officers are trained to respond
the Police will respond as a gun

The police will respond lights
and sirens and come to a screeching halt where your child is
help your child respond appropriately Do not run away They
need no longer have gun in hands They need to
comply with officers instructions to lie down on the ground
the police is essential Police
is a gun I am explaining a scenario that will happen in our area
again kids will be war in the common
grounds Share this with your children tell this story

we will keep our community safe

TRAYVON TRIPTYCH

I. George Zimmer Presses the Mute Button

They say I was angry
The same country that promotes
drunks and pot heads to President

The same eleven o'clock
news that shows sobering
views of Trayvon in his hoodie

next to sketches of the same height
weight race under the crawl of "Still at Large"
They talk about the bar fights

remind me of domestic charges and police exams
So what if I am angry?
Or thought I was

cause I never saw anger till
I saw that kid's fists
and I don't know how you get so much at so young

but he could have punched a sink hole the size of Florida
with enough chains he could have dragged the entire nation into the sea

II. Conversion of a Bullet

I weigh the same as seven Skittles
a hundredth of an Arizona tall ice tea
In a fraction of a second

I am faster than cable news commentary
can outrun any child's cry
but most of my life is spent

confined in a chamber
jammed metal to metal with my brothers
shivering in the same nightmare

Will it hurt when the hammer falls?
What happens when the trigger's released?
Imagine my relief after the fire

when I felt the warmth of human flesh
nestled in the boy's chest
found rest in a ready-made womb

What should I care whose life I devour?
In the flash I was greater than God

III. The Phone Call Trayvon Never Made

Hello? Police?
There's a white man following me
and I think he's got a gun

trying to do me like Malcolm
like Medgar Evers in my own driveway
Drive me away like Assata Shakur

I think she's Tupac's mom
Hello Mom?
I'm not sure but I think I have been sentenced to thug life

Hello Dad?
Did you not have the words to warn me of this much fear?
My phone is dying

My text messages will be used against me in a court of law
My attorney will be appointed to me by a state
That had a slave code before it was a state

No I don't understand the rights you have given to me
No I don't understand why I must remain silent

BULLET CATCH

for Jesus Huerta, Chavis Carter, Victor White III,
three young men of color who committed suicide via gunshot to the head
although all three were handcuffed in a police squad car at the time.[ii]

Step right up! Step right up! Ladies and Gentlemen! Boys and Girls!
Feast your eyes on the brown-tan-black man-boy and the wonder of a life-
time!

Come see the patrol car. Come see the back seat. Come see the folded body the folded boy, the hands folded behind the back. Come see the boy patted down for weapons. Come feel for weapons. Feel arms that can't move. Feel the chest: nothing but breath. Feel the groin: nothing but meat. Even check the teeth.
Check the cuffs: taunt, tight, metal chewing into the wrists.

Check the numbers: .45 caliber, .38 caliber, 22, 21, 17-years-old.

Watch the patrol door open. Watch the boy get jammed in. Watch the hands. Watch the head. Watch the body fold. The handcuffs hold. Watch the chains chew the wrist.

Watch the boy catch the bullet in his teeth. in his jaw. through his eye. in his skull.

You'll never see the gun blast. You'll never see the pistol pulled.
You'll never see the bullet switch or the last phone called made.

Step right up. Step right up. Step out of your house. Step onto the street. Step out of the car, put your hands up, hold your hands out, place them behind your back. You have a right to be shocked into silence. You have a right to tell everyone; they won't believe a thing.

5
The hands are empty
4
The chain is taunt
3
The chamber's loaded
2
The hammer's cocked
1

Want to see it again?

HOW TO STAND UP LIKE ROBERT HAYDEN

See like now a lot of Brothers
Be however they are sporting Mohawks
In skate parks thick-rimmed glasses and elbow
Patches. Brothers be showing love
To Brothers in the club revering Mothers
Openly calling Papa-non-grata. A lot of
Sisters be sporting crop tops banging indie rock
Half head shaven half afro weave dread lock. Taking
Meals at Tavern-on-the-Green and still we
Get screened while shopping shot
For our jackets and jacked-up
By cops and locked up if we cop even
A shot of protest. See if you'd been
Born today and not yesterday you
Could wink right back at Melvin B
Tolson and say I, too, sing Black
American Poet; I can make my line break
Right across U.S.A's ass.

HOW TO GET DOWN LIKE JAMES BROWN

Heh!
One time –huh!
Heh!
Two times – huh! Huh!
This ain't no funeral.

Put your body into it.
They want a fall
but it's the getting up.
Show the world who's boss.
Bring the Earth

to your feet.
Three tines – huh! Huh! Huh!
This ain't no black
and white achieve live
television show. You can't

hear the audience screams
while they can only wish you were talking
to them. They wish they could
comprehend the howls and wails
and whispers in between.

How you be preacher
and creature and *sex*
machine and prey.
How you pray like
paradise on fire

and rise though they be thinking
you are on your knees.
Hit me!
They will claw and yell
for an eighth of your note.

Wish they could dive into your hair
ride the rapids of your brow
drape a cape and soar with your
every step kissing *Please please*
please while you pretend to walk away

while you pretend the spirit
has taken you over
and you can't bear to leave
the stage but that's not how you
and the spirit do.

Clap your hands! Stomp your feet!
In the jungles brothers
In the jungle you were born in the fires
of former plantations.
You know the coldness of lights

on Christmas day.
And they'll say
Hardest working man
While they cut eyes to your feet
And they'll pull

at poppa's new clothes
till they can call them their own
And they'll scream
when you say *Hit me!*
Scream when you say *Hit me!*

scream when you say hit me
and they'll dance their muffled asses
to *Say it Loud!*
twerking and jerking and taking
all the floor pushing you to the corners

to the shadows right to the edge
making you
disappear like the jungles
but *please please please*
please don't go.

Don't leave me in the fader.
Don't run to another track
Don't fall into the quiet
in between *i know you're out there*
Come on clap your hands!

Stomp your feet!
Clap your hands.
Stomp your fee
Clap ya

HOW TO TALK WITH ZORA NEAL HURSTON WHEN NO ONE ELSE CAN HEAR[iii]

Watch your language, your dactyls
and your spondees. She's a trickster
and tricksters be trickling on the tongue
like tuners touching on piano keys. Also
watch for zombies. She had the dead
walking before Kirkman or Romero
or even Matheson was pondering
survival for survival sake. Don't mention
her being naked on the candle altars or
voodoo drums or the giant snake. That's
just research to her. She birthed
Black Feminism when
Janie shot Tea Cake and all the white
women swarm her circle her
claim to protect her but never
realize giving voice to the voiceless
isn't the same as forcing words into
a mouth. Watch your mouth.
Words can go real south real sudden nowadays. They shot
Alesia Thomas when she said something bound up
in the back of a police car. They shot
Renisha McBride when she said she was outside
and she needed some help. They shot
Aiyana Stanley-Jones while she was on the couch
in her grandmother's lap
whispering in her sleep. She was only
seven years old. Ssssh. Listen.
You can hear them grinding
the bones of these women
into the dust of our memoires.
You can hear gardens growing
in the breath of unmarked graves.

HOW TO WALK IN AN AUTUMN EVENING THROUGH A NEIGHBORHOOD THAT'S SAFE

The city trades in its haze
for clearer days and bluer nights

and party-hitters don knit
armor and short skirts grow tights

as fashionable women work smarter
at the art of exposing the body

and flesh-hungry men relearn
how to repress and starve.

And all the bars roll-up
their awnings and serve extra

alcohol to keep warm.
And all the stoop councils

adjourn early and all the anger
that last season swarmed over

a single sizzling comment now
comes to a blustery stop. And even

the cops can't fathom taking out their
hands to grab a random brother

and throw him to the ground feel
around his waist his thighs

his ass and his groin tear
open his pockets watch

whatever coin fall out figure
out they have the wrong one

kick him in the stomach and
tell him “Move along, son.”

MUSIC APPRECIATION

I. Old School

They say before Jordan Davis
was shot and killed by a white man
who went home claimed self-defense and called
for a pizza

Jordan spent
his Monday nights
outside Atlanta
at the discount roller rink

$1 per slice
$1 to skate
one in front and one behind
bounce left bounce right

His mother right there
watching her son glide on through
the world turning beneath his feet

II. Gangsta Rap

They say when Michael Dunn fired nine times
into the car killing Jordan Davis
Dunn saw a gun
But Dunn saw music

the anger in the music

saw it leak into the pavement
make the doors shake
then every widow in the neighborhood started to break
cops came out the woodwork beat everyone

resisting arrest
arrested everyone else they could find
used hair-triggers and tech nines
billy clubs and cat-o-nines

and the blood of the community
was washed with a city hose
then Dunn felt a pulsing
deep in his nose

his eyes started to ache
and the Monster of America
climbed out from an earthquake
Black bodies in its claws

Black bodies in its jaws
and though the beast gave Dunn
only a wink in its wake

that white man drew his gun
and he just shot away

just   shot away

III. Classic Rock n' Roll

They say Merry Clayton lost the baby
after recording the Rolling Stones song

They needed a different sound
a sound like America

but Merry Clayton gave them a sound
that broke its own barrier

folded time into space until
the United States became a black hole

a hologram on its own horizon
a singularity

belting out
a sound beyond the universe

we can conceive
so we only believe we hear

a crack in Merry Clayton's voice
a vacuum in the beat

a darkness so tight
there's space

for neither mother nor child
to cry

HER NAME WAS RENISHA McBRIDE

"Her name was Renisha McBride. She is not just a girl who was murdered on a porch."
–Tina Vásquez [iv].

I.
Heard you had a fight with your parents
Heard you stormed out the front door
vowing never to speak to them again

Heard you had a little to drink that day
smoked a little weed
listened to a little hip-hop

Heard you liked the ladies
liked ladies that were with other ladies
like the hip-hop song goes
Your chick chose me

Heard you took the wrong turn
missed the stop sign
hit the other lady's car

Heard you knocked on his door

II.
Heard his 911 call
I have a woman here and she's been in acci-
-No
There's someone outside trying to break-
-No
"I just shot someone on my front porch."
Yeah that's the one

Maybe he didn't hear you say "help"?
Maybe you didn't say it right?

Needed to enunciate extend your vowels
end in a question a tilted neck a tennis skirt
and a twirl of your blonde hair:
Yeah that's how it's done

Maybe he didn't hear you through the rain

III.
Was it raining?
Was it soaking through the clothes?
beating down on you
like black skin?
Leaving streaks in your eyes
like women left bleeding on the curb?

Did it curse you? Crush you?
Keep you captive like a photograph
with your hat on backwards
and the words in the caption misspelled
for every concerned blogger
or cable channel reporter
to shine it
through the darkness
like a porch light
guiding your way home?

HOW TO DANCE DURING A RIOT

for Michael Brown & Ferguson
for Freddie Gray & Baltimore
for a city near you

Get up
Get on up
Get your hands up

Show 'em up
Put 'em up
Put your hands up

Shake it to the south
To the east
To the west

Put 'em up
Complyin'
Not resisting arrest

Shout demands
To the DJ
James Brown

Motown
Say it loud
Shoot 'em fo he run now

Move the crowd
Do what I say now
Left foot stomp!

Right foot stomp!
Ain't nothing going on
But a peaceful protest

Ain't nothing going on
But civil unrest
Move it

Like a pusher
A pedestrian
A president

Shake it like a stun grenade
Going off in a residence
Shake it like a shake down

Lock up in the Fed
Bounce like a bullet
Off of grandma's head

Get down
Like you doing
What the officer said

Just get back up
Before they think you're dead
Get your hands up

Get your hands up
Get your hands up
Get 'em up

HOW TO GO TO SLEEP

for Aiyana Stanley-Jones
killed by a single bullet during a botched police raid.
She was asleep on the couch at the time.
She was seven years old.

Cycle 1

If you can't fall asleep

Lie down
imagine your toes are asleep
now your ankles now your knees
feel the air by which you breathe
go in and out
Count sheep
but there are no sheep here
then count cracks in the ceiling
cobwebs in the corners
the creaking of the house
the shadows you see move
then the raindrops
then the rose pedals
then your breath

Cycle 2[v]

half the night is spent with half a heart rate
breathing slowed body growing cold
and no dreams
dreams are bad experts say
put a rat on a raft and watch it splash
all night never reaching REM then put him
in front of a cat and watch the rat
stand still in the face of its own death
bad dreams are simulations necessary for survival
but not here
there is only cold slow breath

when seventeen-year-old Je'Rean Blake Nobles needed cold orange juice
he attended to his business as necessary for survival
still Clauncy Owens jumped the curb in his Chevy
shot Je'Rean multiple times at minimum range
on a crowded street
in broad daylight
and everybody watched

Cycle 3[vi]

deep sleep like a house
settling on a street with no streetlamps
and Detroit S.W.A.T. in position
First 48 reality show television crew in tow

but there are no dreams here
no handcuffs
no nightsticks
no submachines
no headphones
no boom stick
no Ka-bars
or black helmets
or black boots
or black outs
or black suits
shotgun shells
shotgun mics
laser sighting
Fresnel light

just delta waves in the mind
delta unit right behind
open window
right outside

reinforced Kevlar
bulletproof vest
rifle recoil
close to the chest
Aiyana is sleeping
quiet on set

Cycle 4

if you see lightning
out the corner of your eye
could you dream of thunder?

if you see lightning out the corner
of your eye
could you dream of thunder?

can you see your grandmother
testify under oath
a truth so deep it can only scream?

can you hear a whole police force
honk in triumph
applaud in thunder?

do you know the ban on assault is over?
mine-resistance vehicle
40 million dollars thick

steel pad battering ram
make the door split
seven-year-olds don't stand a chance

Cycle 5

can you hear it?
can you hear the house settling?
the springs in the couch?
your grandmother's fingers running through your hair?
can you hear it?
a pebble kicked off the pavement
a leaf pressed on wet grass
is that thunder in the neighborhood over?
is it moving closer or farther away?
how soon before it all comes down
can you see it?

can you see the day replay?
the tape rewind?
the nightstick?
the courtroom?
the rat before the cat?
can you see images bleed through?
the orange juice fills the cracks in the ceiling
rose pedals explode from his chest
can you see it?
can you see what's moving faster than your eyes?
see what the eye ain't never really see?
Chauncy and Je'Rean debate policy
on national television. Mertilla Jones at graduation
gives her grandbabygirl a hug.
can you feel this?

you feel this?
there are no dreams here
this is survival strategy
hold it
hold on to it
you're about to wake up.

HOW TO GIVE A EULOGY FOR YOUR THIRD FAVORITE PET

(when ya'll two never really talked much)

The bird
died on the carpet
staring down the staircase
feathers ruffled in wonderment
as if by staring it could unlock the cellar
as if by staring it could hatch an egg of love.

And who doesn't love
eggs? Well, maybe not birds
unless it's their eggs, nested on top of a cellular
tower, kept warm by stolen carpet
samples. Ah, the wonderment
of multiplicity: how a staircase

can be a mountainside or just a staircase
or a metaphor for love;
how the first kiss can ascend you to wonderment
then drop you like a dead bird
on the carpet
next to the cellar

or basement, or whatever. My family never had a cellar.
Our staircase
only went up, but it did have a carpet.
My mother loved
that house "like Beatniks love listening to Byrd."
as she used to say. I wonder what that meant.

And I'm filled with wonderment
that this poem's still going on. Don't you, dear reader, feel locked in a cellar?
Don't you want to be a bird
and fly free, or at least walk up the staircase?
Wouldn't you love
to do something else, like vacuum your carpet?

Wouldn't you rather read a poem that mentions the horrors of carpet
bombs in your tiny villages or the wonderment
of sitting with the one you love
while they announce no indictment for the shooting or hiding in a cellar,
the doors barely holding while a tornado turns your staircase
into a bird?

PLEA

Baby, can we slice our child?
Scratch 'em? Burn 'em?
Emblem 'em at birth?
Slap 'em out the womb with my ring finger?
Give 'em your boxing uppercut?
Mark that kid up!

No broken bones
or severed nerves
just something on the skin?

This country has a history
of taking black and brown children
to prisons
to plantations
to places of higher learning
where they learn a higher hatred
of themselves
twist to higher societies and hide
until no longer seen or sometimes they simply
disappear.

Let's make it clear that won't happen
to our child. Let's sear ourselves
onto the flesh.

Let's carve our initials in the child
like a lover's tree
and yes surely child services will be sure to take 'em
but we can find 'em
and surely we can get 'em back.

EVERY TIME YOU WRITE ABOUT MARISSA ALEXANDER

you end up on vacation.

Every time you write about Marissa Alexander, you start at the same place:
Marissa Alexander's packing her clothes. Rico Gray comes in, gets in her face.
I'm going to kill you, bitch! he screams through the bathroom door.
You're on vacation.

You're on vacation with your family.
You're nine or ten or twelve-years-old staring at the same red carpet the same red walls
Same air-conditioner chilling in the window humming through it all.
Your father stands tall announcing, *Today, you're going to shoot a gun.*

You're on vacation.

Marissa Alexander is able to get to the garage, but automatic door won't engage.
Rico Gray is flying though rage. *I'm going to kill you, bitch!* The door won't open.
Marissa Alexander goes to the glove box and grabs her gun.

You're at the gun range.

You're at the gun range and you're holding a .38
police special – the weight of it holds your whole body down.
It's the lightest gun you can find.
White man comes up from behind
puts his hands over yours saying *Let me help you, son.*

Daughter.
Marissa Alexander just had a daughter.
Preemie. 8 months.
She aims for the wall.

The white man who's not your father at all
says *Let me help you, son*
and wraps his hands around yours so that
it's his hands and the gun
and your hands are no more. You have white-man hands
holding a .38 special flat nose enclosed base.
Hold it steady hold it straight.
Shoot for the black face.

The tin target
the smiling face:
two dots and a curve
scorched dark from a thousand sparks
a thousand shots
a thousand vacationers that come and go
face still smiling though

still saying *C'mon brother, come take a shot*
I dare you. I double dog dare you.
Come point your gun and have a nice day.

Rico Gray
says *If I can't have you, no one will*
flies into rage and threatens to kill
has five baby mamas and beat every last one.
Marissa Alexander cocks the gun.

You pull the trigger.

RHETORIC[vii]

The difference between poetry and rhetoric
is being ready to kill
yourself
instead of your children.
-Audre Lorde "Power"

DON: I want to talk to you

ANN: Now that the Ferguson grand jury documents have been made public

BILL: The looters and arsonists sent a strong message

FOX: And so
Let's talk about race. Let's talk about black-on-black violence.

ANN: Someone's got to say it

RUDY: 93% of blacks

BILL: 99.9 percent of all police

FOX: Americans, 53 percent

ANN: a minimum of 3.3 percent

DON: everybody talking about race,

FOX: just throwing flames on a fire. it's just inappropriate.

RUDY: very disappointing

BILL: I know many African-Americans who are appalled

DON: I didn't want to discuss at length crime in the African-American community or
how to fix other ills that seem to be plaguing the community

ANN: Improving their "economic status" doesn't seem to help.

DON: Because black people, if you really want to fix the problem, here's just five things

that you should think about doing

number five. Pull up your pants.

The one with the really low pants is the submissive one.

FOX: it's a black man in a nice suit selling loosies or whatever they're called

DON: Number four now is the n-word

ANN: neighborhoods[?]

BILL: *The New York Times* [?]

FOX: NYPD [?}

ANN: MSNBC [?}

DON: nigger.

FOX: or whatever they're called

DON: Now number three. Start small by not dropping trash, littering in your own communities.

RUDY: It is the reason for the heavy police presence in the black community.

DON: Number two, finish school.

Stop telling kids they're acting white because they speak proper English.

RUDY: I would like to see attention paid to that that you are paying to this and the solutions to that.

DON: And number one, and probably the most important, just because you can have a baby, it doesn't mean you should.

BILL: There are currently more than 43 million blacks living in the U.S.A.

ANN: That's more black people being murdered,

FOX: Because we cannot ignore that race plays a role in how we police in America.

RUDY: I think we do a pretty good job. Not a perfect job. But the reality is--

FOX: If Eric Garner were a 300-plus-pound white man resisting arrest
the police would have treated him differently.

DON: So, please, black folks, as I said if this doesn't apply to you,

ANN: a cop in Chicago fatally shot an unarmed civilian, LaTanya Haggerty, a
26-year-old computer programmer thought LaTanya had a gun --
but that turned out to be a cellphone.

DON: Pay attention to and think about what has been presented in recent
history as acceptable behavior.

ANN: four New York City police officers shot an unarmed Amadou Diallo,
after he pulled out what looked like a gun. It turned out to be a wallet.

DON: I'm not talking to you.

ANN: Michael Brown gunned down like a dog in the street by Officer
Darren Wilson.

DON: OK. So You can love what I said or you can hate it.

FOX: it's clear that we police people differently in America based on their
economics and ethnicity.

BILL: That should be clear to everyone.

DON: You can love what I said or you can hate it.

FOX: he was saying "I can't breathe, I can't breathe," and not attended to

DON: So
we're going to take a break from the headlines

BILL: the lynch mob

DON: black folks, as I said this doesn't apply to you,
And it's not going to.

FOX: Your
humanity was forgotten

DON: So,   black folks
I'm not talking to you.

FOX: because   black   life   worth less

RUDY: insignificant.

DON: You can love what I said or you can hate it.

ANN: more black people being murdered

DON: Matters not to me.

ALL LINES MATTER[viii]

The New All
A[n] All Love Song
The All Panthers
All Power!
All Art
Let the world be a[n] All Poem
a brief moment / in All History

All and Blue
The All Eyed Peas
Ma Rainy's All Bottom
For All Girls Who Have Considered Suicide // When the Rainbow is Enuf
All Tuxedo
Little All Dress
Heartthrob never, All and ugly as ever / However,
I see a red door and want to paint it all
All Sabbath
The All Album
all-on-all crime

from white hands peeling all skins over / america
the body of one / all man / contains no life
Those four all girls blown up / in that Alabama church
her lynched all boy

The Little All Boy

And I am all, but O! my soul is white
...no lighter / Than an all midnight
So will my page be all that I write? // Being me, it will not be white. / But it
will be / a part of you

you'll sit down and say "The All..."
The all wrestles with the superman.
...the all driver, and in / back the man and the woman, / usually young and
always white.
And their allness [becomes] apparent, that one first...
hates, instead, him self / him all self

But
I love you all! // I love all // Because all are me

But all shouldn't be [/] scared of revolution

HOW TO BUILD A PRISON

for Philadelphia, USA

1.

Always hated that building and never knew why
The one right before the on ramp for 95
Cross-corner from the statue of Tamanend
Riding the world-turtle stretching out his hand

William Penn got along with the Indian
That's why it's not Fort Philly
That's why there's no wall
But there's this building

Five stories tall all boarded-up
windows and blackened red brick
A corner where Philadelphia starts to unfold
A block where the City of Brotherly Love sold slaves

2.

MOVE[xi]: 1 city, 2 stories

They lived like animals	*They wore dread locks*
They ate garbage	*They grew organic fruit*
They shot from the bunker	*There were no guns in the house*

Rebroadcast on Chanel 10
The bomb the blaze the heat
That which we all agree
MOVE: one neighborhood, 2 survivors

3.

Rebroadcast on Chanel 10
Every year the police helicopter
releases the bomb like New Year's Day
releases Mummers on Broad Street

Follow it like City Hall Scandal
Follow it like Eagles-Cowboys game
Follow it like 4th quarter Hail Mary
going… going… going…

4.

The security guard locks doors like forgotten trauma
I'm in my office late grading papers that analyze poems
that protest against policy
I'm in my office marking in red when students misspell "Sanchez"

The security stops to remind me
Every Liberal is a Conservative
that hasn't been mugged yet
He was a cop before I was born

back when Philly was a Police Force
Crack a head through a windshield
in order to protect
Light a block on fire to serve

5.

Order a cheesesteak
in South Philly
Notice the sign
ORDER IN ENGLISH ONLY

Notice a T-shirt
for sale HELP
PUT MUMIA SIX FEET
CLOSER TO HELL

Go across the street
Notice the sign
OWNER DOES NOT ACCEPT
BILLS COVERED IN BLOOD

6.

My students ask me if I
will take a haunted tour
of historic Eastern State Penitentiary
I tell them *As a Black man*
I try to never set foot in a prison
I tell them
I live in Philadelphia
I already have bars on my door

WANTED:

KIDS FROM SUBURBIA

ASSEMBLE FROM THE TRAIN STATION TO THE MARKET & MALLS OF URBAN AMERICA!

SHOUT FROM THE BASE OF YOUR GUT OF YOUR BOWELS LIKE YOU MEAN IT!

STAND UP FOR THE RIGHTS OF PEOPLE YOU DON'T KNOW!

TAKE ON BIG BUSINESS BEFORE BIG BUSINESS TAKES ON YOU!

MEET SOMEONE?

FIGHT FOR YOUR RIGHT TO SLEEP GUILT-FREE AT NIGHT!

PROTEST WORLD HUNGER BY RATTLING YOUR JEWELRY.

WE ARE ASSATA

We are braces and birthdays
weekend barbeques
commuter traffic
and job interviews

beauty salon barber shops
the doorbell on a first date
healthcare homeless vets
rising murder rate

We are "Killer Wanted"
We are post no bail
come home honey
go directly to jail

We are warning lynchings
and church fire bombs
charred black child
cross in her palm

We are eating at the counter
We are staying in our seat
cracks in our head
burns on our feet

from street protest and bus boycotts
while grandma in the kitchen *don't you stir no pot*
and grandpa in his bottle *it's all for not*
still we march on arms in a lock

or hands on the car hood stopped by law
frisking our skins with a delicate claw
like master on the selling block bearing us all
auctioning out our womb selling off our balls

We are history
economy nickel and dime
We are the blackness of gravity
and the burden of time

We are animals
animus spirit and soul
We are the fossil fuels
that make things go

the strike that slow the garden hoe
the quiet cry *no means no*

We are the crooked beaker the combative preacher
smart street sweeper and the secret teacher

the car that roll on the investigation go on
the Medgars the Emmetts the Seans and Travons

We are Assata Shakur
We are America too
and if you're reading this
we are you

KNIVES OF PEACE

for Sonia Sanchez
with apologies to Sonia Sanchez

yeah my sista
where are the knives of peace
the swords of peace
ready to go to war for peace
soldiers of peace
generals of peace
vanguard apache zulu warriors of peace
bloods of peace
crips of peace
got mine with a tech 9 extra clip of peace
napalm of peace
hydro bomb of peace
thermo nuclear multiple warhead of….

sorry?

Oh, you mean knife and fork of peace?
like plate of peace?
like the slice of pizza I just ate for dinner
for peace?

why are you trying to do that?
why are you trying to feed the world
when half of America's overweight
and the other half can't feed ourselves?

why are you trying to cure our cancer?
why you trying to heal our heads?
why you talking all peace?
don't you know all that peace talk spreads?

get peace in the streets
get peace in the schools
then all the kids start thinking peace is cool

start putting peace all on Youtube
then it spreads to TV
hour-long special brought to you by drug companies
whose side effects include mild heart disease
wobbly knees
and massive migraines every time you sneeze
and you want us to swallow this pill called peace?
sista, please

peace ain't buying no car
peace ain't paying no bills
peace ain't supplying those knockoff thrills
we crave in the cry of the night
and when we try to holiday from everyday plight
peace gets stopped at security
            makes us miss our flight
that ain't right.

this ain't no time for peace
or peace marches
or protests in the park
by old heads to throw all these army recruiters off their mark
or talk to have men in dark suits knocking on the door

asking *whatcha writing?*
who you teaching?
who's talking this peace
we want names

nah, this is end game
end days
time to pull down the shades
blow a little haze
and watch ourselves kill ourselves on TV

no peace for you no peace for me

time to cut the throats of killers and victims alike
and we might not get our peace
by at least we'll have
our silence.

HOW TO BE BLACK IN AN AIRPORT WITH YOUR INDIAN WIFE

First I button up my professor vest –
my why-yes-I-am-an-African-American-Professor-vest -
 I'm not a real professor. Technically I teach part time.
Later, in line, I unbutton my vest, place my belt in the scanner
(so now my pants are sagging), and all my paper and pens
(now I can't read or write) and take a deep breath
because this is where I worry about my wife.

See, this ain't no well-lit café or high-end retail store.
This ain't a cool summer breeze on white concrete.
My wife's not trying to keep from stomping her feet
fearing an open-air argument with a Black man is an open call for cops
to come throw me to the ground, cuff my throat, grind the sidewalk
into my ear all of which hasn't actually happened yet
but if it did

I'd probably still lose that argument.

Nah, this ain't it.

The TSA checks and rechecks my wife's I.D.
asks her to remove her sari
(though it's a Ralph Lauren trench coat) and unwrap her chunni
(a Marc Jacob scarf) then scoff in silence
at our stuff as they push us on through and even though
these post 9-11lines ain't hardly nothing new and even though
the whole ordeal last like maybe a minute or two and even though
it takes longer for me to hop across carpet and re-lace my shoe I swear

when it comes to my wife
even the body scanner seems to grow
more suspicious: it's sweeping bar slows
to trace her every inch and curve
as if the darkness of her hair could decompress the cabin;
as if the desi of her skin could turn the sky to ash.

All this to say
I'm sorry,

Baby, this was supposed to be our revolution
love song, but the only real turbulence we face
is in the air with everybody else. The plane shakes
me awake, your grip tightens around my hand.
I turn to you and say Nina, please understand
I am not three fifths of an economy class,
your Punjabi needs not to be patted-down.
Those are concerns for the ground
with the Dotbusters and killer cops
the race-doubters and the follow-me shops.
Here we are 33A and 33B.
Fly or fall we are free.
And you can trust me Baby
because I'm your husband, I love you,

and I'm a professor.

HOW TO LIGHT YOUR OWN POEM ON FIRE

Eric's smoking a cigarette as the protest marches by.

Tanisha drops her groceries on the concrete.

The mounted television replays Rodney

while the speakers blast Marvin *What's Going On?*

Trayvon's looking at the candy.

Latasha's in the freezer for O.J.

Running through the aisles

John and Tamir play with their toy guns.

The cashier ask Amadou how he'd like to pay.

On the way out Emmett offers me a wink

so quick in a step it is gone.

This is our world

burning to no conclusion

in a smolder no word can blow out.

THE TALK

When two people love each other
or think they love each other
or think they see love in someone
else   they will try to be alone
together   which is better than being alone
by yourself   unless you loan your self out to others
in which you might not get your self
back   so
when you find someone of interest
show interest in getting closer
while cautious not to come off too strong
or too easy so   give them space
keep your eyes down in fact
just cross to the other side of the street
people may see you as threat or suspect and
when they see you as a suspect
keep your eyes down put your hands
up say yes sir and no sir and I'm going
to reach into my pocket and take out
my I.D. sir and no sir I do not have a weapon
cause you are a weapon your mind and body and
breath are a weapon
and like any weapon you are a piece of art
and like any art they'll want to lock you up
behind glass and look at you and never
ever touch you and all you want to be
all we all want to be is touched   so
when you find someone you want
to touch and who'll want to touch you back
make sure you hear words like honey
and sweetie and pumpkin pie and
beau but not so much
that you don't hear them from anyone
special   and not so much that you don't believe them

when heard and not so much that they turn
into words like jezebel and black
bastard and fucking
faggot and goddamn
dyke because these words will come
at night when you are walking alone
on the street grab at your breath take you
from your body and rip away your mind and you are mine
my child or worse still
when you find someone willing
to have a child with you and with you
alone you will know
the cacophony of a clock ticking past
curfew you will know the cold sweat
of an insomnia sheet you will know
the world is your partner limbs over yours
lips to your ear
saying *I will be here*
tomorrow and tomorrow I will
kill everyone you love.

THIS POEM WOULD LIKE TO START WITH "THANK YOU."

This poem appreciates your patience and acceptance even though at this point
you have no idea what this poem is about.

This poem would like to offer you the occasional word count
for your convenience: forty-five and counting
and you are still here. (Thank you.)

This poem wants to shake your hand
wants to pat you on the shoulder
is resisting the urge to offer a full embrace
just in case you're not comfortable with that.

This poem does not want to get too personal.
Doesn't want to unravel like a thread
off your jacket, wants to ask "Hey
where'd you get that jacket?" not "Why you always dress
so clean?" or "What do mean America?
Where are you really from?" and no
"C'mon, you have to be mixed." No
this poem does not want to do this.

This poem wants to be a happy poem
offer you a smile hoping you'll offer
a smile back. (if not, that's fine) Why attack you with words?
- one hundred seventy-one and counting -
Still having fun?
Okay

this poem won't even mention security

like the guards in front of libraries that need to see your i.d. or a new friend that hears you speak and decides your hometown must be white or the white boy that dresses like a flyboy and says to your face *i'm trying to look more jive* or the five officers looking for a suspicious character and need to see your i.d. or the roommates when something breaks and you're the one always left with the broom or the elevator in the conference hall where people pause even though *come in, there's plenty of room* or the cops that can't believe you teach here and need to see your i.d. in order to keep the neighborhood safe and just to be safe

this poem won't even mention sex
so please dismiss any reference to strangers encroaching in the dancehall
cause you're moving and smiling and alone and so tall
and so strange so exotic and something to kiss
to caress to feel to grind and play
for a night or a song then push you away.

This poem will say nothing
of any fetishes or obsessions or psychic scars
left by microaggressions you may still carry
like that time you went to visit
your fair-hair friend in a straight comb town

and barely preteens you two found
some random yard sale and while thumbing through books
and records and whatever was there
some white-shadow woman noticed your nappy
black hair and leaned in behind you
close to your ear whispering
"Need a basketball?"

This poem won't mention that at all.

no

this poem wants to convey silence
or violence

silence being the most violent word
this poem knows.

this poem will now go.

HOW TO COOK A FISH

Step 1:
When gutting the fish
slip the knife into the head
from the back of the throat.

The eyes don't blink so
neither should you. Instead
think about your great –

grandfather coming back
from the war. He never
talked about cutting his

comrades or dulling under
Jim Crow. He would just come
home silently and gut fish.

Step 2:
When cooking the fish
grill in a pan mixed
with peppers or fry

on a bed of onions until smoke
becomes a cloud of unwanted
kisses and the sizzle

becomes a noose.
Remember your grandmother.
No protest

song can save you.
Remember you still have
the knife.

Step 3:
When devouring the fish
do not dine like your
father. Sip wine

across an Atlantic
of friends. Cherish the corner
kisses and mixed table

blessings. Love the
kaleidoscope of faces
and know that one of them

will betray you
while the rest sit back
and watch.

NOTES

i. Erasure from City of Fenton Facebook post "Kids will be Kids" December 4, 2014 (removed the same day)
www.cbsnews.com

ii. Victor White III, 22, died in police custody in Iberia Parish, Louisiana March 3, 2014. Death ruled a suicide.
Chavis Carter, 21, died in police custody in Jonesboro, Arkansas July 28, 2012. Death ruled a suicide.
Jesus Huerta, 17, died in police custody in Durham, North Carolina November 19, 2013. No charges filed.

iii. Alesia Thomas - 1977-2012. Mother of two, struggled with mental illness. Beat (not shot) by a LAPD police officer in abdomen, thighs, and groin several times while restrained in the back of a patrol car. When questioned under oath, the partner of the arresting officer could not offer a clear for Alesia's arrest.

Renisha McBride – 1994-2013. Survived a car accident in Dearborn, Michigan. Killed via shogun when she knocked on stranger's door for help. The homeowner, a 55-year-old white man, says he felt threatened. In high school, Renisha was on the cheerleading squad.

Aiyana Mo'Nay Stanely-Jones – 2002-2010. Can be seen in a photo smiling against a background of Disney princesses. She was shot by a member of the Detroit S.W.A.T. team. The S.W.A.T. team raided the wrong house.

iv. Facebook post. November 2013.

v. On May 14, 2010 - Je'Rean Blake, 17, was shot and killed by Chauncey Owens on a crowded street in broad daylight.

vi. On May 16, 2010 Detroit S.W.A.T. team entered the house of Aiyana Stanely- Jones looking for Chauncy Owens (who lived upstairs) with The *First 48* realty show television crew in tow.

vii. Found text from rush transcripts:

Ann Coulter "Would it Kill You to Hire More Black Cops? (Yes)", August 27, 2014. Accessed December 10, 2014. *anncoulter.com*

Megyn Kelly "Former NYC Police Commissioner, Brooklyn President on Controversy Over Cop's Takedown" *The Kelly File*, December 5, 2014. Accessed December 9, 2014 *foxnews.com*

Don Lemon "Problems The Black Community Faces; Don Lemon's Suggestions" CNN Newsroom, July 27, 2013. Accessed December 9, 2014. *edition.cnn.com*

Bill O'Reilly "What the Ferguson Protesters Accomplished" *The O'Reilly Factor*, December 02, 2014. Accessed December 9, 2014. *foxnews.com.*

Ian Schawrtz "Fireworks: Giuliani vs. Michael Eric Dyson: 'White Police Officers Won't Be There If You Weren't Killing Each Other 70% Of The Time'" November 23, 2014. Accessed December 9, 2014. *realclearpolitics.com.*

viii. Lines appropriated from Alain Locke, Paul Lawrence Dunbar, Amiri Baraka, Nicole Lovebreed, Claudio Segovia, Hector Orezzoli, August Wilson, Ntosake Shange, Biggie Smaills, The Rolling Stones, Jay-Z, Sonia Sanchez, Lucille Clifton, Michael S Harper, Elizabeth Alexander, William Blake, Sterling A Brown, Langston Hughes, Nikki Giovanni, Derek Walcott, Charles Bukowski, Wallace Stevens, and The Last Poets.

ix. The MOVE stand-off/bombing, May 13, 1985.
At approximately 5:30 PM, Philadelphia Police drop C-4 from a helicopter unto 6221 Osage Avenue in the mostly African American neighborhood of Cobbs Creek.
61 homes razed.
250 people rendered homeless.
11 dead.
6 adults.
5 children.

ACKNOWLEDGEMENTS

"Bullet Catch" and "Music Appreciation" first published in *CURA*, no. 16 (2015): http://curamag.com/issues/2015/12/4/2-poems-1.

"Every time you write about Marisa Alexander" first published in Red Sky: *poetry on the global epidemic of violence against women*, edited by Melissa Hassard, Gabrielle Langley, and Stacy Nigliazzo, 110-111. Greensboro, N.C: Sable Books, 2017.

"How to Build a Prison" first published in Mumia and Mass Incarceration Forum. ed. Tanisha C Ford. *The Feminist Wire*. January 22, 2014: https://thefeministwire.com/2014/01/how-to-build-a-prison-a-poem/.

"ssssh" first published as "Untitled (ssssh)" *Runes* Winter Solstice (2003): 102.

"The Talk" first published in *North American Review*, 301, No. 1 (2016): 26.

"This poem would like to start with 'Thank you'" first published in *African Voices*. Summer (2017): 28.

"Trayvon Triptych" first published in Mumia and Mass Incarceration Forum ed. Tanisha C Ford. *The Feminist Wire*. January 25, 2014: https://thefeministwire.com/2014/01/trayvon-triptych-a-poem/.

"Wanted" first published in *Stray Dog*, no . 5 (2005): 4.

"We are Assata" first published in Celebrating Assata Shakur and the Black Radical Tradition. ed. Hakima Abbas. *The Feminist Wire*. July 16, 2013: https://thefeministwire.com/2013/07/we-are-assata/.

The Author would like to extend gratitude to the following:

Lamont B Steptoe, Dr. Joyce A Joyce, Larry Robins, Cave Canem, Natalie Diaz, Bridggett M Davis, Tanisha C. Ford, Marci Blackman, Sundays @ Branded, Glitter Pomegranate,

Professor Phillips, Professor Nelson, Professor Imbriglio, Professor Terry-Morgan,

Matthea Harvey, Victoria Redel, Jeffrey McDaniel, Cathy Park Hong, D Nurkse, Kamila Aisha Moon,

Sarah Gambito, Mariahadessa Ekere Tallie, Bushra Rehman, Cathy Linh Che, VONA, Love Jawns, the Asian American Writers' Workshop, Sarita's Mac & Cheese,

Carolyn A Butts, Metta Sama, Abiodun Oyewole, Tony Medina, Richard Krawiec,

Alicia Garza, Patrisse Cullors, Opal Tometi,

Sonia Sanchez, Patricia Smith, Ed Toney, Ross Gay,

Michael S Harper, Bill Van Wert, C D Wright, Ntosake Shange

Yesenia Montilla, the Honorable JP, Erica Davis, Amazing Grace, Yolanda Wisher, Dr. Sullivan, Mecca Jamilah Sullivan, C&R,

the Sasha that should be here, the Zamani before their time,

the Funeral Home where I learned my laughter, the Funeral Home where I shared my meals, the Funeral Home that protested City Hall and in the basement stored coffins crafted for children,

Mom, Dad, Case, Grand-mom,

and Nina...see you at home.

C&R PRESS TITLES

NONFICTION

By the Bridge or By the River? Stories of Immigration from the Southern Border by Amy C. Roma
Women in the Literary Landscape by Doris Weatherford, et al
Credo: An Anthology of Manifestos & Sourcebook for Creative Writing by Rita Banerjee and Diana Norma Szokolyai

FICTION

A Mother's Tale by Khanh Ha
Last Tower to Heaven by Jacob Paul
History of the Cat in Nine Chapters or Less by Anis Shivani
No Good, Very Bad Asian by Lelund Cheuk
Surrendering Appomattox by Jacob M. Appel
Made by Mary by Laura Catherine Brown
Ivy vs. Dogg by Brian Leung
While You Were Gone by Sybil Baker
Cloud Diary by Steve Mitchell
Spectrum by Martin Ott
That Man in Our Lives by Xu Xi

SHORT FICTION

Fathers of Cambodian Time-Travel Science by Bradley Bazzle
Two Californias by Robert Glick
Notes From the Mother Tongue by An Tran
The Protester Has Been Released by Janet Sarbanes

ESSAY AND CREATIVE NONFICTION

Selling the Farm by Debra Di Blasi
the internet is for real by Chris Campanioni
Immigration Essays by Sybil Baker
Death of Art by Chris Campanioni

POETRY

How to Kill Yourself Instead of Your Children by Quincy Scott Jones
Lottery of Intimacies by Jonathan Katz
What Feels Like Love by Tom C. Hunley
The Rented Altar by Lauren Berry
Between the Earth and Sky by Eleanor Kedney
What Need Have We for Such as We by Amanda Auerbach
A Family Is a House by Dustin Pearson
The Miracles by Amy Lemmon
Banjo's Inside Coyote by Kelli Allen
Objects in Motion by Jonathan Katz
My Stunt Double by Travis Denton
Lessons in Camoflauge by Martin Ott
Millennial Roost by Dustin Pearson
All My Heroes are Broke by Ariel Francisco
Holdfast by Christian Anton Gerard
Ex Domestica by E.G. Cunningham
Like Lesser Gods by Bruce McEver
Notes from the Negro Side of the Moon by Earl Braggs
Imagine Not Drowning by Kelli Allen
Notes to the Beloved by Michelle Bitting
Free Boat: Collected Lies and Love Poems by John Reed
Les Fauves by Barbara Crooker
Tall as You are Tall Between Them by Annie Christain
The Couple Who Fell to Earth by Michelle Bitting
Notes to the Beloved by Michelle Bitting

www.ingramcontent.com/pod-product-compliance
Lightning Source LLC
LaVergne TN
LVHW051017080826
845145LV00009B/2678

* 9 7 8 1 9 4 9 5 4 0 2 0 8 *